Tiny Ted's Telling Tales

From Shelter Pup to Working K9

Vanessa Taylor Tanner

Copyright © 2024 by Vanessa Taylor Tanner
All rights reserved.

No portion of this book may be reproduced in any form without written permission from the publisher or author except as permitted by law.

A special thank you to my best friend and K9 Companion, Taylor "Nugget Man" Tanner. I could not have made it here without you. You may be gone, but your memory will forever live on in my heart and work.

Acknowledgement

A special **thank you** to my husband, Tommy Tanner, who helped me make my dream come true. Thank you to my boss, Chris Wilkinson, owner of Smoky Mountain Process and Legal Services, for believing in me and allowing me a chance. A huge thank you to my mother, Kim Reynolds, who instilled the love of reading in my life, making me the book lover and writer that I am today. A heartfelt thanks goes out to Jackson Animal Care Center and its staff. Lastly, but certainly not least, thank you to my sweet K9, Ted, for being my companion, work partner, protector and rescuer.

Contents

"My First Night in the Shelter" 11

"Where Are We" 13

"What's Next?" 14

"Alone" 15

"Day Two" 17

"Dreaming Again" 19

"Always Left Behind" 20

"Leaving The Shelter" 23

"MY First Big Outing" 24

"Working K9" 26

"A Face To The Voice" 27

"My First Peaceful Night" 28

"My First Night in the Shelter"

It's something I'll never forget. I was found on the streets that day, scavenging for food and wondering where my next meal would come from. Life for a stray can be scary for a pup on his own. I worried if I would have a warm and dry place to sleep that night, and if my belly would be empty when bedtime came. Being a street dog is dangerous and lonely, as not all humans are kind, and many times, I've been run off and shooed away by people. I don't know why, as I mean no harm and just want a bite to eat and a friendly touch.

The day is growing cold and my empty belly growls with hunger. No food yet, just some empty hamburger wrappers. They sure did smell good though, making my tummy even more hungry. The hours tick on through the day, and I miss my momma and siblings. Many of us have been separated along our street journey and have been left to fend for ourselves, and I wonder where they are. As I lost track of the time, looking for food and shelter, a sweet and kind lady in a van suddenly stopped and scooped me up before I knew what was happening. I was a bit scared at first, but she showed such kindness, and I could sense that she meant me no harm. She put me inside her warm van and took me for a ride to somewhere unknown to me at the time. The cabin of the van was warm. I was thankful for the heat on my cold face and little body. She was gentle with me and gave me lots of pets and love throughout the ride. I was so grateful to see her and that she was nice to me. I wondered if she had any food. My belly was so hungry and my eyes heavy and tired. I drifted off for a while, the hum of the motor and heat putting me into a deep well needed sleep.

"Where Are We?"

Suddenly, the van made a turn, and I opened my eyes. I tried to keep a brave face, but I was nervous of what was next to come. Where were we, and what would happen to me now? We pulled into a big building where I could smell and hear other dogs. It was loud and noisy, and I became anxious and scared again. "Brave face," I told myself. "I've been through a lot, and I can handle whatever is about to happen." This kind lady had been so nice to me, so I decided to go with her without giving her any trouble. Maybe she would give me a few morsels of food for my empty tummy. I hadn't eaten all day, and I was tired and weak from hunger.

"What's Next?"

She took me inside, where there were dogs in every corner and crate. They all looked so sad and lonely, like me. I realized that they were also lost souls that had ended up in the same spot I was in. This was the shelter, and I was now a shelter pup. You hear about it, but you don't think it will ever happen to you. The sweet lady who runs the shelter cleaned me up and gave me a bath. I got doggy shampoo and warm water and had a clean coat of fur for the first time ever. She gave me my own bowl with plenty of food and water and a warm place to sleep. I even had a soft, warm blanket to snuggle with. She also gave me shots and preventative medication to keep me and the other pups here safe from germs.

"Alone"

The scariest part of being a shelter dog, is when the staff leaves at night and those cage doors slam shut. You realize you're at the shelter with no family. You don't know how long you may be here or what the future holds for you. There isn't a lot of room in overcrowded animal facilities, so I was put in the isolation area, away from many of the other dogs. The staff does their best, but there isn't a lot of room for us to play and socialize. However, I was so grateful that my belly was full and that I had a warm bed that night. Although, I was still lonely and scared. The noises of the other dogs barking and whining took some getting used to and made me a little restless. I wondered about my mom and siblings again and hoped that they were warm and had full bellies too. As I lay my head down, for my first comfortable night's sleep, I wondered what it would be like to be a family dog, and to have a human of my own.

That night, I dreamed of the day that I would be adopted and wondered how my story would go. Right now, I am grateful to be where I am, but I do feel as though great changes are coming my way soon. I heard a voice that night. It told me to just be patient and to hold on and that my day was coming.

"Day Two"

I slept ok during my first night in the shelter. A new day has come, though and I was still somewhat nervous. The noise and whining of the other pups was a bit much for me, but I rested the best I could. Suddenly, that morning, I could hear humans and smell food, my belly automatically grumbling. I hope they shared some with me. Finally, after all the ruckus, my turn came and a nice kennel handler came to my crate with food and water, all for me! I scarfed it down quickly and enjoyed every morsel! I can't believe I didn't have to hunt for my breakfast this morning.

After mealtime, I got to go out to the yard for potty and playtime and meet some of the other pups. I let the sunshine on my sweet face and enjoyed the breeze as it ran over my freshly clean coat. I made pup and human friends, with my outgoing personality and happy demeanor, willing to play with anyone who's up for the challenge!

As I saw that some of the other dogs had been here for a while, I knew I might be here for quite some time myself. Shelter pups aren't always **wanted** as much as store-bought pups and pure breeds. But, I decided to make the best of it while I'm here and listen to that voice in the back of my head, telling me to "be patient," and that "your time will come."

"Dreaming Again"

The day is winding down and we've all had dinner. I made more friends here today and the staff just loves me and my cute face. I wish they could stay with us all night, but I know they can't. The lights go out and the staff goes home to their own families, once again. I lay my head on my bed, that many dogs before me have used to sleep on. I wonder what it's like to have my own bed, my own toys... my own furever home and human to love. As I close my eyes, I drift off into a land where I have that sweet human, my own home, my own life outside of the shelter. One day, I think to myself, as I doze off into sleep.

"Always Left Behind"

It's been almost two months, and here I am, still at the shelter. I see all of my pup friends getting adoption interviews and finding their furever homes every day. I'm so happy for them to find their own homes and humans and my heart is always full for them. Though, I do often wonder what's wrong with me. Why does no one want me as their pup? I promise I'm a good boy and would do my best to be the perfect dog, for my own family.

I used to get excited when I saw a kennel handler come back to the care area with a leash for a visit with a potential family. But it seems like my day never comes and it's always another dog that someone is interested in. I wonder if my special time will ever come. I decide that my heart is tired, and my appetite is diminishing by the day, as this happens with lots of shelter dogs. It's hard to eat when you're sad. I leave my full food bowl untouched, and I lie down on my used bed, drifting off into a restless sleep. For some reason, I did hear that sweet angel voice in my head again. It said to be patient, as I too, would have a special day.

"March 13th, 2024… Gotcha Day"

Ah, another day of crowded loud kennels and boredom in my crate. Breakfast and fresh water was served by the kennel staff, but I wasn't hungry. I lie down and let the day pass by, as the other dogs bark and whine with anxiety and boredom. The time ticked by, and I tried my best to sleep after we had been taken out for yard and potty time. The day was getting late, and I knew the staff would be leaving for their own families soon. Suddenly, the door to the isolation area opened and a kennel handler came in with a lead. Another adoption interview for one of my lucky friends. But the kennel handler kept passing the other kennels. He kept walking closer and closer to mine. Surely there was a mistake, no one has ever asked for an interview with me. But here he was, leash in hand and opening MY door! I couldn't help but wag my tail and give a small, excited yelp! I was so excited but needed to be on my best behavior so that they could see what a good boy I was.

I walked into the lobby, my little heart racing. I looked over at the most kind and compassionate human I had ever seen. She scooped me up and looked into my eyes. It was love at first sight. There was something about her... I could tell that she was hurting in her heart. That she had recently suffered a great loss. I didn't know what it was exactly, but I knew that it was my job to rescue her. She looked me in my face and asked, "Are you ready to go home?"

I couldn't believe it! A home and human of my very own! The shelter staff cheered and had a small celebration just for me. I had been the pup at the shelter for the longest, and finally my special day came.

I bid farewell to all of my shelter friends, hoping that they too, would find a family soon.

"Leaving The Shelter"

My new owner, Vanessa, carried me out of the shelter doors, holding me tightly in her arms. I had dreamed of this moment. I never wanted her to let me go. She settled us in the cab of her car.

She held me the whole way and watched me adoringly. I couldn't take my eyes off her. My big GOTCHA DAY finally came. She took pictures of us together, posting them on her social media, to show how proud she was of me! Then, she started crying and I wasn't quite sure why. I would understand all of that later though.

"My First Big Outing"

As we left the shelter, Mom was excited and told me that we were going to stop at the Big Chain Pet Store close by. I had never been to a real Pet Store before. I could barely contain my excitement. When we arrived, Mom secured me in a basket. Because it was my very first outing and I showed a small amount of anxiety with my excitement.

We walked over toward the big store, the breeze caressing my face, the sunshine so bright and warm on my skin. I still couldn't believe I was here. I had a beautiful, kind human doting all on me. This was the dream, the moment I had waited so long for.

As we walked into the wonderland of toys and treats, I was amazed at how many new and untouched toys there were on the shelves. My nose could smell them all, and my tail began to wag. They had huge dog bones, toys galore, dental chews, and even doggy cookies! Mom stopped and let me take a whiff and I got to pick out lots of my very own treats. I chose a big rubber bone, a peanut butter ball, lots of bacon treats and of course the cookies. I got my very own stuffed animal to love on and lots of tennis balls. She even outfitted me with my own collar, vest, and training lead.

We made our way to the back of the store to where the beds were. I was in absolute awe of how many beds there were on the shelves. My friends at the shelter would give anything for one of these. Mom took me out of the basket and began to let me sniff and choose. I was so excited, I tried one bed after another. I laid on the softest, most comfy bed I had ever had the privilege of sitting on. Mom must have saw how much I enjoyed it, because she picked it up and put it into our basket and sat me on it.

Was it mine now? Was this comfy bed all for me?! Oh wow! I sure felt like one lucky pup. We stopped to look at clothes and shirts, as Mom said I just had to have my own wardrobe.

We picked out the most stylish of shirts and hoodies, and all of a sudden mom's phone rang. "It's The Boss," she said and took the call while I patiently waited.

Mom's an Investigative Process Server for Smoky Mountain Process & Legal Services. She handles some pretty neat and important cases. After being on her call for a few minutes, she turned and gave me a wide-eyed look... I could tell by her body language that something exciting had happened.

"Working K9"

Mom still had a surprised, but proud look on her face, when she reached down to snuggle me. "Ted, she informed me... You're now the newest Investigative Process Server and my work partner! You're now a Working K9! My amazing boss Chris Wilkinson said you can start immediately! Your first assignment is tomorrow, and rigorous training begins immediately."

Bewildered did not begin to explain my feelings. I started my day as a shelter pup and now just a few hours later, I had my own human, a home, bed, toys of my own, and now a JOB! Talk about a miracle! We finished up at the pet store, picking up the best of pet foods and a road travel kit for my new job. We headed out and to the car where mom secured me safely and then looked at me and said, "Time to go home and meet the rest of the Pack, buddy." Oh, what music to my ears. A home with other pups for me to play with! I felt like I'd won the lottery.

"A Face to the Voice"

When we made it to our new home, I got to sniff around the yard and find my own potty spot. Mom was proud of me and gave me a treat for a job well done. We walked in the front door and the first thing I saw was a table with a photograph of an older, very handsome dog. The name "Taylor" was etched on the frame.

Taylor, Beloved Best Friend ~ 05/01/08-09/15/25

I knew who he was immediately. He was the voice that I kept hearing in the shelter, telling me to be patient and that my time would come. I saw Mom look at his photo with sadness and adoration. I finally understood. He was no longer with her but must have crossed that beautiful Rainbow Bridge. I also realized that my job was not just a working K9, but to help heal this kind human's heart. I had never been more honored or privileged before. It was in that moment, that I decided to be the best boy ever for her. I stood there and made a silent vow to her beloved companion Taylor, that I would watch over her until they meet again.

"My First Peaceful Night"

After I had met my pack members and had my belly full of good food, fresh water, and treats, Mom got me ready for bed. She got all of my gear out for work the next morning, so that we didn't have to rush when it was time to leave. Apparently working dogs don't get to sleep in much. I was ok with that, and so excited for my first day of work tomorrow. Mom put my new bed on the floor next to hers, but she didn't put me into it. Instead, she laid me in her big bed and allowed me to sleep next to her all night. It was the best night of rest either one of us have had in months. I was finally home.

Be sure to follow our next "Tiny Ted's Telling Tales," to learn about the life of an Investigative Process Pup, the trial and errors of work and some good, pure fun.

About the Author

From Shelter Pup to working K9, watch Ted and his exciting work adventures and shenanigans as a Jr. Investigator. He and his human, Vanessa, are always on the go, looking for the next big task. You will see Ted grow and learn, as he undergoes top-notch K9 training and receives lots of love and knowledge from his new owner. Ted's life may have started out hard and in the streets but see him living his best life now!

www.ingramcontent.com/pod-product-compliance
Lightning Source LLC
Chambersburg PA
CBHW040020130526
44590CB00036B/32